PRE-APPRENTICESHIP
MATHS & LITERACY FOR
TILING

Graduated exercises and practice exam

Andrew Spencer

A+ National Pre-apprenticeship Maths & Literacy for Tiling
1st Edition
Andrew Spencer

Publishing editor: Sarah Lang
Project editor: Aynslie Harper
Proofreader: Katharine Day
Text designer: Miranda Costa
Cover designer: Aisling Gallagher
Cover image: Shutterstock/Gajus
Permissions researcher: Karen Forsythe
Production controller: Emma Roberts
Typeset by: Q2A Media
Reprint: Katie McCappin

Any URLs contained in this publication were checked for currency during the production process. Note, however, that the publisher cannot vouch for the ongoing currency of URLs.

© 2016 Cengage Learning Australia Pty Limited

For product information and technology assistance,
in Australia call **1300 790 853**;
in New Zealand call **0800 449 725**

For permission to use material from this text or product, please email
aust.permissions@cengage.com

ISBN 978 0 17 047451 1

Cengage Learning Australia
Level 7, 80 Dorcas Street
South Melbourne, Victoria Australia 3205

Cengage Learning New Zealand
Unit 4B Rosedale Office Park
331 Rosedale Road, Albany, North Shore 0632, NZ

For learning solutions, visit **cengage.com.au**

Printed in Australia by Ligare Pty Limited.
1 2 3 4 5 6 7 26 25 24 23 22

A+ National
PRE-APPRENTICESHIP
Maths & Literacy for Tiling

Contents

LITERACY		

MATHEMATICS		

Introduction

It has always been important to understand, from a teacher's perspective, the nature of the mathematical skills students need for their future, rather than teaching them 'textbook mathematics'. This has been a guiding principle behind the development of the content in this workbook. To teach maths that is *relevant* to students seeking apprenticeships is the best that we can do, to give students an education in the field that they would like to work in.

The content in this resource is aimed at the level that is needed for students to have the best possibility of improving their maths and literacy skills specifically for trades. Students can use this workbook to prepare for an apprenticeship entry assessment, or to even assist with basic numeracy and literacy at the VET/TAFE level. Coupled with the activities on the NelsonNet website, https://www.nelsonnet.com.au/free-resources, these resources have the potential to improve the students' understanding of basic mathematical concepts that can be applied to trades. These resources have been trialled, and they work.

Commonly used trade terms are introduced so that students have a basic understanding of terminology that they will encounter in the workplace environment. Students who can complete this workbook and reach an 80 per cent or higher outcome in all topics will have achieved the goal of this resource. These students will go on to complete work experience, do a VET accredited course, or will be able to gain entry into VET/TAFE or an apprenticeship in the trade of their choice.

The content in this workbook is the first step to bridging the gap between what has been learnt in previous years, and what needs to be remembered and re-learnt for use in trades. Students will significantly benefit from the consolidation of the basic maths and literacy concepts.

Every school has students who want to work with their hands, and not all students want to go to university. The best students want to learn what they don't already know; and if students want to learn, then this book has the potential to give them a good start in life.

This resource has been specifically tailored to prepare students for sitting apprenticeship or VET/TAFE admission tests, and for giving students the basic skills they will need for a career in trade. In many ways, it is a win–win situation, with students enjoying and studying relevant maths for work, and for Trades and Registered Training Officers (RTOs) receiving students who have improved basic maths and literacy skills.

All that is needed from students is patience, hard work, a positive attitude, a belief in themselves that they can do it and a desire to achieve.

About the author

Andrew graduated from SACAE Underdale in 1988 with a Bachelor of Education. In 1989, Andrew went on to attend West Virginia University, where he completed a Master of Science (specialising in teacher education), while lecturing part-time.

In 1993, Andrew moved to NSW and began teaching at Sydney Boys' High, where he taught in a range of subject areas including Mathematics, English, Science, Classics, Physical Education and Technical Studies. His sense of practical mathematics continued to develop with the range of subject areas he taught in.

Andrew moved back to South Australia in 1997 with a diverse knowledge base and an understanding of the importance of using mathematics in different practical subject areas. He began teaching with the De La Salle Brothers in 1997 in South Australia, where he continues to work and teach today. Andrew has worked in collaboration with the SACE Board to help develop resources for mathematics with a practical focus.

In 2011, Andrew was awarded the John Gaffney Mathematics Education Trust Award for valuable contributions to the teaching of Mathematics in South Australia. Andrew received a Recognition of Excellence for outstanding contributions to the teaching profession by CEASA in both 2011 and 2012 and, in 2014, he was one of 12 teachers from across Australia to work in collaboration with the Chief Scientist of Australia to develop a better understanding of the role of mathematics in industry. As part of this role, he undertook research in this area, spent time working with the industry and then fed the results back to the Chief Scientist.

Andrew continues to develop the pre-apprenticeship and vocational titles, based on mathematics and literacy, to assist and support the learning of students who want to follow a vocational career path. He is currently working towards the nineteenth title in this series. The titles have also been adapted in the UK and Asia, as the importance of this type of functional mathematics continues to grow. All schools have students who will follow a vocational pathway and it continues to be a strong focus of Andrew's to support the learning needs of these students.

Author Acknowledgements

For Paula, Zach, Katelyn, Mum and Dad.

To the De La Salle Brothers for their selfless work with all students.

To Dr Pauline Carter for her unwavering support of all Mathematics teachers.

To all students who value learning, who are willing to work hard and who have character … and are characters!

LITERACY

Unit 1: Spelling

Short-answer questions

Specific instructions to students

- This is an exercise to help you to identify and correct spelling errors.
- Read the activity below and then answer accordingly.

Read the following passage, and identify and correct the spelling errors.

> To get the best results from your tiling work, it is important to prapare the surface beforehand. Irespective of the type of surface that you are tiling, the surface needs to be level, clean and, importently, clear of dust and debris particals. Floor surfaces are usualy either concrete or timber, while plastarboard is most comonly used for walls. Priyor to tiling, a few things should be considered, such as has the concrete been cured for a minnimum of 28 days?
>
> Steel-trowelled concrete should be roughaned and thorughly washed before tiling or there may not be suficient adhesion. Concrete releese agents and curing compounds should be removed by mechanical means. If cracks have appeared, they need to be filed and prepared to ensure a smooth surfice remains.
>
> It is generaly recomended that ceramic tiles are never adhered to timber floors. Untreeted floors should be primmed and then allowed to dry, leading up to tiling. Plasterboard is a paper surface and needs to be waterproofed before tiling. Tiling over plasterboard generally involves adhering tiles to the paper surface. If the plasterboard is suseptible to any form of moisture, it may deteriorete.

Incorrect words:

_____

_____

Correct words:

_____

_____

Unit 2: Alphabetising

Short-answer questions

Specific instructions to students

- In this unit, you will be able to practise your alphabetising skills.
- Read the activity below and then answer accordingly.

Put the following words into alphabetical order.

Chalk line	Adhesive
Underlay	Levelling compounds
Floor tiles	Tile spacers
Grout	Tile nippers
Grout spreader	Adhesive applicator
Scissors	Cutting tool
Stanley knife	Straight edge
Level	Scoring tool
Soft cloth	Sponge

Answer:

_____

_____

_____

_____

_____

_____

_____

_____

_____

_____

_____

_____

_____

_____

_____

_____

_____

_____

9780170474511

Short-answer questions

Specific instructions to students

- This is an exercise to help you understand what you read.
- Read the following activity and then answer the questions that follow.

Read the following passage and answer the questions in full sentences.

Every tiler knows that tiles have to be cut to fit to a wall or floor space. In some cases, tiles also need to be cut into different shapes and sizes. Cutting tiles becomes easier with the use of appropriate equipment and with practice. When cutting tiles, allow a few extra tiles to practise on.

There are a few options to consider when cutting tiles. If a tiler is working on a number of tiling projects, a tradesman's tile cutter will make completing the projects easier. Some specialist tile companies hire out tile cutters. Or another option is to purchase a cheaper tile cutter.

When a tiler is working out how to make a straight cut on a tile, he uses a pencil to mark where the tile needs to be cut. It is important to cut the tile smaller than the space to be tiled, so as to allow for even and well-spaced grout joints. Once marked, the tile is placed in the tile cutter and the scorer is run across the tile (only once). This creates a breaking point in the tile. A clean and accurate cut is made by pushing down the breaker.

QUESTION 1

What makes cutting tiles easier?

_____

QUESTION 2

What are some 'options' to consider when cutting tiles?

_____

_____

QUESTION 3

Why should tiles be cut smaller than the space being tiled?

_____

QUESTION 4

What does the tiler use to mark a straight line on the tiles?

_____

QUESTION 5

What does the scorer 'create' across a tile?

_____

Shutterstock/Nagy-Bagoly Arpad

MATHEMATICS

Unit 4: General Mathematics

Short-answer questions

Specific instructions to students

- This unit is designed to help you to improve your general mathematical skills.
- Read the following questions and answer all of them in the spaces provided.
- You may not use a calculator.
- You need to show all working.

QUESTION 1

What unit of measurement is used to measure:

a   a wall area for tiling?

Answer:

_____

b   the amount of grout required?

Answer:

_____

c   the amount of adhesive required?

Answer:

_____

d   the size of a tile?

Answer:

_____

e   the dimensions for a tile cutter?

Answer:

_____

f   the length of a glass or tile drill bit?

Answer:

_____

g   the cost of a tile scriber?

Answer:

_____

QUESTION 2

Give examples of how the following might be used in the tiling industry.

a   percentages

Answer:

_____

b   decimals

Answer:

_____

c   fractions

Answer:

_____

d   mixed numbers

Answer:

_____

e   ratios

Answer:

_____

f   angles

Answer:

_____

QUESTION 3

Convert the following units.

a 1.2 metres to cm and mm

Answer:

___

b 4 tonne to kg

Answer:

___

c 260 centimetres to mm

Answer:

___

d 1140 mL to litres

Answer:

___

e 1650 g to kilograms

Answer:

___

f 1.8 kg to grams

Answer:

___

g 3 metres to cm and mm

Answer:

___

h 4.5 L to millilitres

Answer:

___

QUESTION 4

Write the following in descending order.

0.4   0.04   4.1   40.0   400.00   4.0

Answer:

___

QUESTION 5

Write the decimal number that is between:

a 0.2 and 0.4

Answer:

___

b 1.8 and 1.9

Answer:

___

c 12.4 and 12.5

Answer:

___

d 28.3 and 28.4

Answer:

___

e 101.5 and 101.7

Answer:

___

QUESTION 6

Round off the following numbers to two (2) decimal places.

a 12.346

Answer:

___

b 2.251

Answer:

___

c 123.897

Answer:

___

d 688.882

Answer:

___

e 1209.741

Answer:

___

QUESTION 7

Estimate the following by approximation.

a $1288 \times 19 =$

Answer:

_____

b $201 \times 20 =$

Answer:

_____

c $497 \times 12.2 =$

Answer:

_____

d $1008 \times 10.3 =$

Answer:

_____

e $399 \times 22 =$

Answer:

_____

f $201 - 19 =$

Answer:

_____

g $502 - 61 =$

Answer:

_____

h $1003 - 49 =$

Answer:

_____

i $10001 - 199 =$

Answer:

_____

j $99.99 - 39.8 =$

Answer:

_____

QUESTION 8

What do the following add up to?

a $4, $4.99 and $144.95

Answer:

_____

b 8.75, 6.9 and 12.55

Answer:

_____

c 650 mm, 1800 mm and 2290 mm

Answer:

_____

d 21.3 mm, 119.8 mm and 884.6 mm

Answer:

_____

QUESTION 9

Subtract the following.

a 2338 from 7117

Answer:

_____

b 1786 from 3112

Answer:

_____

c 5979 from 8014

Answer:

_____

d 11 989 from 26 221

Answer:

_____

e 108 767 from 231 111

Answer:

_____

QUESTION 10

Use division to solve the following.

a $2177 \div 7 =$

Answer:

___

b $4484 \div 4 =$

Answer:

___

c $63.9 \div 0.3 =$

Answer:

___

d $121.63 \div 1.2 =$

Answer:

___

e $466.88 \div 0.8$

Answer:

___

The following information is provided for question 11.

To solve using BODMAS, in order from left to right, solve the **B**rackets first, then **O**f, then **D**ivision, then **M**ultiplication, then **A**ddition and lastly **S**ubtraction. The following example has been done for your reference.

EXAMPLE

Solve $(4 \times 7) \times 2 + 6 - 4$.

STEP 1

Solve the Brackets first: $(4 \times 7) = 28$.

STEP 2

No Division so next solve Multiplication: $28 \times 2 = 56$.

STEP 3

Addition is next: $56 + 6 = 62$.

STEP 4

Subtraction is the last process: $62 - 4 = 58$.

FINAL ANSWER:

58

QUESTION 11

Use BODMAS to solve the following.

a $(6 \times 9) \times 5 + 7 - 2 =$

Answer:

___

b $(9 \times 8) \times 4 + 6 - 1 =$

Answer:

___

c $3 \times (5 \times 7) + 11 - 8 =$

Answer:

___

d $6 + 9 - 5 \times (8 \times 3) =$

Answer:

___

e $9 - 7 + 6 \times 3 + (9 \times 6) =$

Answer:

___

f $6 + 9 \times 4 + (6 \times 7) - 21 =$

Answer:

___

Unit 5: Basic Operations

Section A: Addition

QUESTION 1

Shutterstock/Robert Kneschke

A tiler checks the perimeter of a bathroom floor that is to be tiled. The sides measure 2 m, 5 m, 3 m and 5 m. What is the total length of the perimeter?

Answer:

QUESTION 2

An outdoor area is to be tiled and the sides, or perimeter, of the area measure 5 m, 8 m, 13 m and 15 m. What is the total length of the perimeter?

Answer:

QUESTION 3

Four pallets of ceramic floor tiles are delivered to a worksite. Each pallet has 720 tiles. How many tiles have been delivered?

Answer:

QUESTION 4

A tiler and his apprentice complete several jobs over four weeks. They travel 282 km in the first week, 344 km in the second week, 489 km in the third week and 111 km in the fourth week. How many kilometres have they travelled in total, over the four weeks?

Answer:

QUESTION 5

Over a month, a major tiling company delivers the following number of pallets of ceramic floor tiles: 32 in the first week, 47 in the second week, 57 in the third week and 59 in the fourth week. How many pallets of tiles have been delivered in total?

Answer:

QUESTION 6

An apprentice buys a 6.5-mm glass and tile drill bit for $22, two pairs of safety glasses for $16 and two pairs of gloves for $9. How much has the apprentice spent?

Answer:

QUESTION 7

A specific job requires mosaic ceramic tiles. The tiler already has the tiles but they are in four different lots. If the first lot has 70 tiles, the second lot has 90 tiles, the third lot has 40 and the fourth lot has 100 tiles, how many tiles does the tiler already have, in total?

Answer:

QUESTION 8

A tiler is contracted to complete the grout work on an apartment. She uses one 20-kg bag of construction grout on the kitchen, one 10-kg bag of coloured grout on the bathroom and one 15-kg bag of coloured grout on the laundry. How many kilograms of grout does she use in total?

Answer:

_____

QUESTION 9

A client wants to get some indoor and outdoor areas of a home tiled. The areas include $16\,m^2$ for a bedroom, $18\,m^2$ for an outdoor pool area, $8\,m^2$ for a laundry and $11\,m^2$ for a bathroom. How many square metres are to be tiled in total?

Answer:

_____

QUESTION 10

A tiling company uses the following number of decorative tiles on different kitchen jobs: 178 on the first job, 188 on the second job and 93 on the third job. How many tiles are used in total?

Answer:

_____

Section B: Subtraction

Short-answer questions

Specific instructions to students

- This section is designed to help you to improve your subtraction skills for basic operations.
- Read the questions below and answer all of them in the spaces provided.
- You may not use a calculator.
- You need to show all working.

QUESTION 1

A tiler has 103 ceramic floor tiles that measure $450\,mm \times 450\,mm$ on a pallet. At different stages of the tiling job, the tiler uses 52 tiles, then 12 tiles, then 13 tiles, and lastly, 11 tiles. How many floor tiles are left on the pallet?

Answer:

_____

QUESTION 2

A warehouse has 500 bags of tile adhesive in stock. If 250 bags are delivered to a tiling company in one week, and a further 125 bags are delivered the following week, how many bags remain at the warehouse?

Answer:

_____

QUESTION 3

If 243 decorative tiles are used in one week and 159 are used in the next week, how many more were used in the first week compared to the second week?

Answer:

_____

QUESTION 4

If $27\,m^2$ of a hospital floor is to be tiled using $300\,mm \times 300\,mm$ antimicrobial tiles, in an area that totals $90\,m^2$, how many square metres remain?

Answer:

_____

QUESTION 5

A tile laser level retails for $108. The store manager offers a discount of $17. How much does the customer pay?

Answer:

_____

9780170474511

QUESTION 6

A supervisor of a major tiling company orders $5000 of personal protection equipment (PPE) for employees. If $2756 is spent on safety boots, long pants and long-sleeved shirts, how much has been spent on the remaining safety gear?

Answer:

QUESTION 7

An area on a building plan totals $96\,m^2$. The client wants $44\,m^2$ to be used for lawn, $17\,m^2$ to be used for gardens and the rest of the area to be tiled with terracotta textured tiles. How many square metres are left to be tiled?

Answer:

QUESTION 8

An apprentice uses 69 20-kg bags of tile adhesive over a period of time. If 105 bags were in storage to begin with, how many are left?

Answer:

QUESTION 9

The odometer of a work van has a reading of $56\,089\,km$ at the start of the year. At the end of the year it reads $71\,101\,km$. How many kilometres have been travelled during the year?

Answer:

QUESTION 10

Shutterstock/Lilyana Vynogradova

A tiling company uses 31 4-L containers of heavy-duty tile and grout cleaner in the first month, 29 containers in the second month and 103 containers in the third month. If there were 250 containers in storage to begin with, how many are left?

Answer:

Section C: Multiplication

Short-answer questions

Specific instructions to students

- This section is designed to help you to improve your multiplication skills for basic operations.
- Read the following questions and answer all of them in the spaces provided.
- You may not use a calculator.
- You need to show all working.

QUESTION 1

A tiler charges $48 per hour. How much is earned for a 45-hour week?

Answer:

QUESTION 2

An apprentice counts 14 750-g wall tile adhesive containers on a pallet. How many containers would there be on 15 pallets?

Answer:

QUESTION 3

A tiler uses 13 litres of diesel for one trip to a worksite, where tiling needs to be completed inside and outside of a client's house. How much fuel is used if the van makes the same trip each day for 18 days?

Answer:

_____

QUESTION 4

It takes 12 310-mL tubes of premixed tile adhesive to complete the ensuite in one house at a new housing development. How many tubes are used to complete the ensuites for all 24 houses of the housing development?

Answer:

_____

QUESTION 5

An apprentice uses 33 bags of premix wall tile adhesive in a week. How many bags does she use over four weeks?

Answer:

_____

QUESTION 6

A tiler uses 16 tubes of 250-g tile adhesive and grout in a week. How many tubes are needed for 15 weeks?

Answer:

_____

QUESTION 7

A labourer's car uses 9 litres of LPG every 100 km. How much LPG is used for 450 km?

Answer:

_____

QUESTION 8

If 673 containers of 4-L white flexible tile adhesive are used per month by a major tiling company, how many containers are used over a year?

Answer:

_____

QUESTION 9

If a labourer uses eight 454-g spray tile adhesive containers each day, how many are used during a 31-day month?

Answer:

_____

QUESTION 10

A small business gets a contract in the country and the workers need to travel to the worksite. If they travel at 110 km/h for five hours, how far have they travelled?

Answer:

_____

Section D: Division

Short-answer questions

Specific instructions to students

- This section is designed to help you to improve your division skills for basic operations.
- Read the questions below and answer all of them in the spaces provided.
- You may not use a calculator.
- You need to show all working.

QUESTION 1

A labourer works a total of 24 hours over three days. How many hours are worked each day?

Answer:

_____

QUESTION 2

A tiler earns $868 for working a five-day week. How much is earned per day?

Answer:

_____

9780170474511

QUESTION 3

Shutterstock/Yunava1

To complete a range of tiling jobs at four different worksites, 140 containers of 4-L premixed tile adhesive are needed. How many 4-L containers are used at each site if they all need the same amount of tile adhesive? Are there any containers left over?

Answer:

_____

QUESTION 4

A tiler's work van covers 780 km in a five-day week. On average, how many kilometres per day have been travelled?

Answer:

_____

QUESTION 5

A company requires 88 20-kg powder tile adhesive bags to finish some tiling work on four separate worksites. How many bags are allocated evenly to each worksite?

Answer:

_____

QUESTION 6

A building supervisor gets paid $2926 for seven days of work, including overtime for the weekend. How much does he earn per day?

Answer:

_____

QUESTION 7

A worker at a tiling company counts 2326 5-kg bags of grout. If the bags are stocked in 100 bag lots, how many lots are there? Are there any bags left over?

Answer:

_____

QUESTION 8

A manager orders 408 bags of 5-kg off-white tile cement for a building company. If the bags are put into six-bag lots at the warehouse, how many lots are there?

Answer:

_____

QUESTION 9

Ninety-six 275-g tubes of sand tile silicone are distributed to 12 different worksites? How many tubes are distributed to each site?

Answer:

_____

QUESTION 10

A supervisor travels 2290 km in 28 days, inspecting worksites. On average, how many kilometres are travelled each day?

Answer:

_____

Section A: Addition

QUESTION 1

If an apprentice purchases a 4-L container of carpet and cork adhesive for $56.75, a 1-L container of vinyl adhesive for $18.85 and a 4-L container of tile and grout sealer for $46.75, how much is spent in total?

Answer:

QUESTION 2

A tiling contractor purchases a rubber tiling mallet for $19.95, a pair of knee pads for $29.95, a 6-inch tile saw with blade for $18.55 and a spirit level for $19.45. How much money is spent?

Answer:

QUESTION 3

A square metre of 450 mm × 450 mm grey ceramic floor tiles costs $29.85, a square metre of 59 mm × 297 mm textured tiles costs $42.50 and a 12-mm glass and tile drill bit costs $39.65. What is the total cost?

Answer:

QUESTION 4

A contractor buys a four-piece multifunction tiling tool for $79.90, three tile sponges for $8.96 and a tile breaker for $19.40. What is the total cost for all of the items?

Answer:

QUESTION 5

An apprentice tiler buys the following tools for her first tiling toolkit: a curved tile nipper for $18.45, a 20-m tile line laser for $253.39 and a grout tool for $28.75. What is the total cost?

Answer:

QUESTION 6

To get to his jobs, an apprentice travels 65.8 km, 36.5 km, 22.7 km and 89.9 km. What is the total distance travelled?

Answer:

QUESTION 7

What is the total length of an outdoor area that measures 15.5 m by 17.8 m?

Answer:

9780170474511

QUESTION 8

Shutterstock/Johann Helgason

A tiling company wants to upgrade their equipment and decides to purchase a new 800W electric tile bridge saw for $470.50, a 1250-mm wet tile saw for $3790.95 and a diamond-grit hole saw set for $249.75. How much does the company spend to upgrade?

Answer:

QUESTION 9

Three invoices are issued for three completed tiling jobs. The first invoice is for $1450.80, for the first job. The next invoice is for $1130.65, for the second job, and the final invoice is for $2660.45, for the last job. What is the total for all three invoices?

Answer:

QUESTION 10

An apprentice purchases a six-piece masonry drill bit set for $34.92, a grout joint finisher for $3.25, a 63-mm diamond blade for $21.95 and a 240-mm magnetic stubby level for $22.35. What is the total cost for these items?

Answer:

Section B: Subtraction

Short-answer questions

Specific instructions to students

- This section is designed to help you to improve your subtraction skills when working with decimals.
- Read the questions below and answer all of them in the spaces provided.
- You may not use a calculator.
- You need to show all working.

QUESTION 1

At the beginning of the day, a bag has 500 T-shaped 1.5-mm spacers. If an apprentice uses 33 spacers over the day, how many remain in the bag?

Answer:

QUESTION 2

An unopened bag has 500 T-shaped 3.0-mm spacers. If 27.5 spacers are used, how many remain in the bag?

Answer:

QUESTION 3

A tiling contractor completes a job and charges $2789.20. The boss of the company gives a discount of $75.50 to the client for being a regular customer. How much does the client need to pay?

Answer:

QUESTION 4

A labourer works 38 hours in a week and earns $729.98. Petrol costs for the week come to $48.85. How much money is left?

Answer:

QUESTION 5

A 410 mm × 80 mm chisel spade bit is purchased for $29.95. If a $50 note is used to make the purchase, how much change is given?

Answer:

QUESTION 6

An apprentice buys two powder-coated square notch trowels. One is 4 mm and the other is 8 mm. Both cost $11.15 each. How much change is given from $30.00?

Answer:

QUESTION 7

A small tiling business has an account balance of $4000.95. If five boxes of 5-kg coloured grout are purchased for a total of $110.50, how much money is left in the account?

Answer:

QUESTION 8

A 15.5 mm section is cut from one side of a 330 mm × 330 mm floor tile to fit on a bathroom floor. What is the size of the tile after the cut?

Answer:

QUESTION 9

A tiling company has $5000 in the work account. The manager purchases a 1200-mm spirit level for $56.90, a 500W 170-mm wet tile cutter with folding legs for $229.95 and six 178-mm tile saw blades for $149.70. How much money is left in the account?

Answer:

QUESTION 10

A tiler gets paid $2280.50 for a fortnight's work. If $350.90 is spent on buying new tools, $44.50 on petrol and $175.50 on food, how much money does the tiler have left?

Answer:

Section C: Multiplication

Short-answer questions

Specific instructions to students

- This section is designed to help you to improve your multiplication skills when working with decimals.
- Read the questions below and answer all of them in the spaces provided.
- You may not use a calculator.
- You need to show all working.

QUESTION 1

Decorative choc-mix marble tiles measuring 300 mm × 300 mm × 8 mm are priced at $19.45 each. If three are purchased, what is the total cost?

Answer:

QUESTION 2

A 65 mm × 200 mm mosaic tile costs $6.25. Thirty are needed to complete tiling work in a bathroom. What is the total cost?

Answer:

QUESTION 3

An apprentice spends $86.55 in a tiling store for three weeks in a row. How much has been spent in total?

Answer:

QUESTION 4

Six 250 mm × 500 mm beige ceramic tiles are bought for $5.08 each. What is the total cost?

Answer:

9780170474511

QUESTION 5

To finish work in a laundry, three 300 mm × 50 mm brown and cream tiles are purchased for $11.75 each. What is the total cost?

Answer:

QUESTION 6

A contractor works for a tiling company and earns $37.55 per hour. If 38 hours are worked in one week what is the gross wage (before tax)?

Answer:

QUESTION 7

A tiler purchases 25 1000 mm × 1000 mm standard charcoal carpet tiles for $24.95 each. What is the cost?

Answer:

QUESTION 8

A tiling company's van has a 52-litre fuel tank. Unleaded fuel costs $1.35 per litre. How much does it cost the driver to fill the tank if there are only two litres left in it?

Answer:

QUESTION 9

A tiling company purchases 14 6.7-kg containers of all-tile adhesive kits for $56.20 each. What is the total cost?

Answer:

QUESTION 10

Agefotostock/Phovoi R./Panther Media

An apprentice tiler earns $160.65 per day. What is the gross weekly wage (before tax) for five days of work?

Answer:

Section D: Division

Short-answer questions

Specific instructions to students

- This section is designed to help you to improve your division skills when working with decimals.
- Read the questions below and answer all of them in the spaces provided.
- You may not use a calculator.
- You need to show all working.

QUESTION 1

Two 4-L containers of under-tile waterproofing costs a total of $170.80. How much does each container cost?

Answer:

QUESTION 2

Four 1-L tile and grout sealer containers for waterproofing cost a total of $70. How much does each container cost?

Answer:

QUESTION 3

A tiling company charges $3732.70 to complete some tiling work during a renovation for a client. If it has taken 50 hours to complete the job, what is the rate per hour, inclusive of labour and materials?

Answer:

QUESTION 4

A tiler charges a client $1577.00 for working a 38-hour week. What is the hourly rate?

Answer:

QUESTION 5

How many 350 mm × 350 mm tiles are needed to fit one line of a 2.4-m long wall?

Answer:

QUESTION 6

An outdoor area is being tiled using 600 mm × 600 mm tiles. If one side measures 12.8 m, how many tiles are needed to tile the side?

Answer:

QUESTION 7

Seven 5-L containers of rapid waterproofing agent costs a total of $612.50. How much does each container cost?

Answer:

QUESTION 8

Nine square metres of a house are being tiled using 200 mm × 200 mm black matt internal floor tiles. The total cost for the tiles is $197.55. What is the cost per square metre?

Answer:

QUESTION 9

amanaimages/© George Gutenberg/Beateworks

An outdoor entertainment area, measuring 24 m², is being tiled using 400 mm × 400 mm beige external floor tiles. The total cost for the tiles is $476.40. How much is the cost of the tiles per square metre?

Answer:

QUESTION 10

A tiling company purchases 45 m² of 450 mm × 450 mm olive stone pattern internal floor tiles for $697.50, during a sale. How much do the tiles cost per square metre?

Answer:

9780170474511

Section A: Addition

QUESTION 1

$\frac{1}{2} + \frac{4}{5} =$

Answer:

_____

QUESTION 2

$2\frac{2}{4} + 1\frac{2}{3} =$

Answer:

_____

QUESTION 3

An apprentice puts $\frac{1}{3}$ of a 20-kg bag of grout powder into a bucket that has water in it. Another $\frac{1}{3}$ of the bag is added because the mix is too watery. How much of the 20-kg bag has been added to the bucket, as a fraction?

Answer:

_____

QUESTION 4

An apprentice adds 1 and $\frac{2}{3}$ bags of grout powder to a bucket with water. Another 1 and $\frac{1}{4}$ bags is added. What is the total amount of grout powder added, as a fraction?

Answer:

_____

QUESTION 5

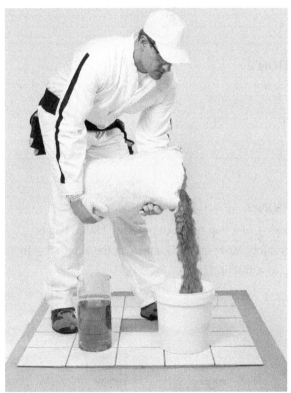

Shutterstock/CSImagemakers

A tiler mixes $\frac{1}{3}$ of a bag of grout powder in a bucket with water. Another $\frac{1}{2}$ of the bag is added. How much grout powder has been used, as a fraction?

Answer:

_____

Section B: Subtraction

Short-answer questions

Specific instructions to students

- This section is designed to help you to improve your subtraction skills when working with fractions.
- Read the questions below and answer all of them in the spaces provided.
- You may not use a calculator.
- You need to show all working.

QUESTION 1

$\frac{2}{3} - \frac{1}{4} =$

Answer:

QUESTION 2

$2\frac{2}{3} - 1\frac{1}{4} =$

Answer:

QUESTION 3

A tiler has $\frac{2}{3}$ of a bag of grout powder. Half a bag is used for a job. How much is left from the original $\frac{2}{3}$ in the bag, as a fraction?

Answer:

QUESTION 4

Shutterstock/B Brown

A 20-kg bag of grout powder is $\frac{3}{4}$ full. If $\frac{1}{8}$ is used on a job, how much is left, as a fraction?

Answer:

QUESTION 5

There are 2 and $\frac{1}{2}$ bags of grout on site. If 1 and $\frac{1}{3}$ bags are used for a job, how much is left, as a fraction?

Answer:

Section C: Multiplication

Short-answer questions

Specific instructions to students

- This section is designed to help you to improve your multiplication skills when working with fractions.
- Read the questions below and answer all of them in the spaces provided.
- You may not use a calculator.
- You need to show all working.

QUESTION 1

$\frac{2}{4} \times \frac{2}{3} =$

Answer:

QUESTION 2

$2\frac{2}{3} \times 1\frac{1}{2} =$

Answer:

9780170474511

QUESTION 3

A subcontractor has five half-full 20-kg bags of tile adhesive. How many full bags does this make, as a fraction?

Answer:

_____

QUESTION 4

There are 8 and a $\frac{1}{2}$ containers of tile adhesive on a pallet at a worksite, which need to be moved using a forklift. If each container weighs 20 kg, how many kilograms are there in total?

Answer:

_____

QUESTION 5

A labourer works 37 and a $\frac{1}{2}$ hours in a week and gets paid $22.50 per hour. How much is earned for the week?

Answer:

_____

Section D: Division

Short-answer questions

Specific instructions to students

- This section is designed to help you to improve your division skills when working with fractions.
- Read the questions below and answer all of them in the spaces provided.
- You may not use a calculator.
- You need to show all working.

QUESTION 1

$\frac{2}{3} \div \frac{1}{4} =$

Answer:

_____

QUESTION 2

$2\frac{3}{4} \div 1\frac{1}{3} =$

Answer:

_____

QUESTION 3

A 5-kg bag of coloured grout is divided into four equal parts before being mixed. How much grout is in each part, as a fraction?

Answer:

_____

QUESTION 4

If an apprentice has a 10-kg bucket of tile adhesive and needs six equal parts for different tiles, how much adhesive is this, as a fraction?

Answer:

_____

QUESTION 5

A labourer carries 20 kg of grout, over three trips, to a dining area and kitchen area. How many kilograms are carried in each trip, as a fraction?

Answer:

_____

Unit 8: Percentages

Section A: Calculating extra tiles for breakages/cutting/possible wastage

EXAMPLE

You've been asked to add 10% more tiles to a job that requires 45 tiles, to account for breakages and/or waste.

To find 10% of 45, add a decimal one place to the left. Therefore, 10% more is an extra 4.5 tiles (rounded up to 5).

10% of 45 + 5 = 50 tiles in total.

QUESTION 1

A tilting company orders stone floor tiles that are 450 mm × 450 mm to complete work for a client. The tiler estimates that 22 tiles are needed for a section of the bathroom floor, but needs to add 10% extra for breakages. How many tiles are needed in total?

Answer:

_____

QUESTION 2

A tiling company orders textured internal floor tiles that are 330 mm × 330 mm to complete work for a client. The tiler estimates that 97 tiles are needed for a dining area, but needs to add 10% extra for breakages. How many tiles are needed in total?

Answer:

_____

QUESTION 3

To complete work for a client, 300 mm × 600 mm tiles need to be used. The tiler estimates that 148 tiles are needed, but needs to add 10% extra for breakages. How many tiles are needed in total?

Answer:

_____

QUESTION 4

A tiler needs 247 black marble self-stick tiles that are 457 mm × 457 mm to complete a job. How many tiles should be ordered, including an extra 10%?

Answer:

_____

QUESTION 5

A tiling company orders 488 tiles that measure 200 mm × 52 mm for work at a housing estate. An extra 10% of tiles is added to the order. How many tiles are ordered, in total?

Answer:

_____

QUESTION 6

Minima matt ceramic floor tiles that are 450 mm × 450 mm cost $37.50 for a packet of six. The tiler completing the job estimates that 72 tiles are needed. How many packets need to be bought, including a 10% allowance for breakages?

Answer:

_____

_____

_____

QUESTION 7

Black Ceramic Floor tiles that are 300 mm × 3000 mm cost $49.90 for a packet of 15. The tiler completing the job estimates that 260 tiles are needed for a dining room and lounge area. How many packets need to be bought, including a 10% allowance for breakages?

Answer:

_____

_____

_____

QUESTION 8

A client has selected nut matt floor tiles that are 400 mm × 400 mm to be laid in three bedrooms, the kitchen and lounge room. The tiles cost $35.95 for a packet of seven. The tiler estimates that 355 tiles are needed. How many packets need to be bought, including a 10% allowance for breakages?

Answer:

_____

_____

_____

QUESTION 9

amanaimages/© Trevor Richards/Abode/Beateworks

A client who owns a townhouse has selected porcelain sandstone matt floor tiles that are 330 mm × 330 mm to be laid in the laundry, kitchen, lounge and dining rooms. The tiles cost $42.20 for a packet of 11. The tiler estimates that 222 tiles are needed. How many packets need to be bought, including a 10% allowance for breakages?

Answer:

_____

_____

_____

QUESTION 10

A client wants the outdoor alfresco area of her café to be tiled using 600 mm × 300 mm grey porcelain sandstone floor tiles. The tiles cost $32.90 for a packet of five. The tiler estimates that 425 tiles are needed. How many packets need to be bought, including a 10% allowance for breakages?

Answer:

_____

_____

_____

Section B: Percentages and purchasing

Short-answer questions

Specific instructions to students

- In this section, you will be able to practise and improve your skills in working out percentages.
- Read the questions below and answer all of them in the spaces provided.
- You may not use a calculator.
- You need to show all working.

10% rule: move the decimal one place to the left to get 10%.

EXAMPLE

10% of $45.00 is $4.50.

QUESTION 1

A hardware store offers 10% off the price of a suction-cup tile holder, which usually retails for $10.00. How much does it cost after the discount?

Answer:

QUESTION 2

A hardware store offers 10% off the price of a 12-mm diamond tile drill bit, which is usually priced at $17.00.

a   How much is the discount worth?

Answer:

b   What is the final cost?

Answer:

QUESTION 3

The regular retail price of a 38-mm diamond tile hole cutter is $52.90. A store has a '10% off' sale. How much does it cost during the sale?

Answer:

QUESTION 4

A 1240-mm pro series tile cutter costs $695. How much does it cost after the store takes off 20% during an end-of-financial-year sale?

Answer:

QUESTION 5

A 1500W 10-kg chipping hammer costs $329 and a long-handled grout scrubbing brush costs $21.90. How much do they cost after the store takes off 20% for both items during an end-of-financial-year sale?

Answer:

QUESTION 6

A tiler purchases five 10-L water-based undercoat containers for $795.00 each. A trade discount of 10% is given. What is the final cost?

Answer:

QUESTION 7

A tiler purchases the following tools at a '10% off' sale: a 28-mm to 93-mm adjustable hole cutter for $33.85, a grout gun for $51.90 and a 10-mm notched adhesive trowel for $13.50.

a   What is the total cost of all the tools *before* the 10% discount?

Answer:

b How much money has been saved from the discount?

Answer:

QUESTION 8

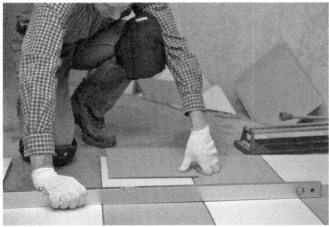

Shutterstock/Lilyana Vynogradova

An apprentice purchases some personal protective equipment (PPE) gear at a '20% off' end-of-financial-year sale. This includes a pair of rubber safety gloves for $25.50, a pair of deluxe hard-shell knee pads for $37.95 and a pair of clear-lens safety goggles for $19.99.

a What is the total cost *before* the 20% discount?

Answer:

b How much money has the apprentice saved from the discount?

Answer:

QUESTION 9

A self-levelling cross-line laser level for floor tiling costs $63.50 after 30% has been taken off.

a What was the original price?

Answer:

b How much has been saved from the original price?

Answer:

QUESTION 10

An apprentice tiler goes to a '15% off' sale and buys a 280 mm × 140 mm polyurethane float for $15.95, a 10-mm diamond-coated hole saw for $15.50, a 125-mm diamond-blade cutting tool for $29.95, a 75-mm tile spreader for $7.50 and a 185 mm × 125 mm × 50 mm grouting sponge for $13.35. How much has the apprentice saved by purchasing the tools at the sale?

Answer:

Short-answer questions

Specific instructions to students

- This unit is designed to help you to improve your skills and to increase your speed in converting one measurement unit into another.
- Read the questions below and answer all of them in the spaces provided.
- You may not use a calculator.
- You need to show all working.

QUESTION 1

How many millimetres are there in 1 cm?

Answer:

QUESTION 2

How many millimetres are there in 1 m?

Answer:

QUESTION 3

How many centimetres are there in 1 m?

Answer:

QUESTION 4

The length of a bathroom wall is 2550 mm. What is the length in metres?

Answer:

QUESTION 5

The width of a bathroom floor measures 3650 mm. How many metres is this?

Answer:

QUESTION 6

The length of one section of a patio is 2.6 m. How many millimetres is this?

Answer:

QUESTION 7

One section of an outdoor entertainment area is 2850 mm in length. Another section is 3250 mm in length. What is the total length of the outdoor entertainment area?

Answer:

QUESTION 8

Three internal areas of a house need tiling: the lounge room, which measures 32.45 m², the dining room, which measures 23.15 m², and a bedroom, which measures 11.85 m². What is the total area, in squared metres, to be tiled?

Answer:

QUESTION 9

What is the length of a tiled path that has the measurements of 2580 mm along the front section, 3250 mm along the side section and 2400 mm along the back of the house? Answer in millimetres and metres.

Answer:

QUESTION 10

An apprentice tiler is reading from a building plan and considers four areas for tiling. He estimates that the square metres for the first area measure $12.85\,m^2$, the second area measure $12.35\,m^2$, the third area measure $12.85\,m^2$ and the fourth area measure $23\,m^2$. What are the total square metres required according to these estimates?

Answer:

Shutterstock/yuttana jeenamool

Unit 10: Measurement

Section A: Area

> Area = length × breadth and is given in square units
>
> $= l \times b$

QUESTION 1

The dimensions of a bedroom floor are 3.5 m × 3.8 m wide. What is the total area?

Answer:

QUESTION 2

An ensuite floor measures 2.2 m × 3.3 m. What is the total area?

Answer:

QUESTION 3

The floor area for a dining room measures 3.5 m × 3.65 m. What is the total area?

Answer:

QUESTION 4

A toilet floor measures 2.1 m × 0.8 m. What is the total floor area to be tiled?

Answer:

QUESTION 5

A bedroom measures 3.3 m × 3.5 m. What is the total area?

Answer:

QUESTION 6

A kitchen wall measures 3.55 m × 0.38 m. What is the total area to be tiled?

Answer:

QUESTION 7

The measurement of an outdoor area is 6.5 m × 3.5 m. What is the total area to be tiled?

Answer:

QUESTION 8

A patio area measures 5.5 m × 4.2 m. What is the total area?

Answer:

QUESTION 9

Shutterstock/bikeriderlondon

An outdoor entertainment area measures 5.2 m wide × 8.6 m long. What is the total floor area?

Answer:

_____

QUESTION 10

An entertainment area adjacent to a swimming pool is 9.5 m long × 2.6 m wide. What is the total floor area?

Answer:

_____

Section B: Costings

Short-answer questions

Specific instructions to students

- This section is designed to help you to improve your skills and to increase your speed in calculating costings.
- Read the questions below and answer all of them in the spaces provided.
- You may not use a calculator.
- You need to show all working.

This is a two-step process. The first step is to calculate the area. The second step is to work out the basic costing for laying tiles per square metre.

QUESTION 1

A lounge room measures 4 m × 6 m and the client wants to use 200 mm × 200 mm brown matt-finish internal floor tiles priced at $21.95 per square metre. What is the total cost for the tiles?

Answer:

_____

QUESTION 2

A wall next to a pool and spa measures 3 m × 9 m and the client wants to use 300 mm × 300 mm cream subtle stone tiles priced at $18.95 per square metre. What is the total cost for the tiles?

Answer:

_____

QUESTION 3

A bedroom measures 3.5 m × 4.5 m and the client wants to use 400 mm × 400 mm white patterned floor tiles priced at $17.95 per square metre. What is the total cost for the tiles?

Answer:

_____

QUESTION 4

A living room measures 6.5 m × 5.5 m and the client wants to use 450 mm × 450 mm beige stone pattern internal floor tiles priced at $14.50 per square metre. What is the total cost for the tiles?

Answer:

_____

QUESTION 5

A laundry wall measures 1.65 m × 4.75 m and the client wants to use 597 mm × 297 mm porcelain tiles priced at $42.50 per square metre. What is the total cost for the tiles?

Answer:

QUESTION 6

Shutterstock/MiloVad

A bathroom wall measures 2.5 m × 4.5 m and the client wants to use 200 mm × 50 mm decorative wall tiles priced at $34.50 per square metre. What is the total cost for the tiles?

Answer:

QUESTION 7

An outdoor area measures 6.75 m × 6.5 m and the client wants to use 810 mm × 406 mm natural stone tiles priced at $84.95 per square metre. What is the total cost for the tiles?

Answer:

QUESTION 8

An outdoor entertainment area measures 7.5 m × 6.5 m and the client wants to use 610 mm × 305 mm natural stone tiles priced at $64.95 per square metre. What is the total cost for the tiles?

Answer:

QUESTION 9

A patio area measures 8.75 m × 7.75 m and the client wants to use 600 mm × 300 mm white limestone floor tiles priced at $74.95 per square metre. What is the total cost for the tiles?

Answer:

QUESTION 10

A pergola area measures 11.25 m × 5.55 m and the client wants to use 600 mm × 600 mm engineered stone tiles priced at $37.95 per square metre. What is the total cost for the tiles?

Answer:

9780170474511

Section C: Advanced costings

Short-answer questions

Specific instructions to students

- This section is designed to help you to improve your skills and to increase your speed in calculating the amount of tiles required for a job.
- Read the questions below and answer all of them in the spaces provided.
- You may not use a calculator.
- You need to show all working.

Calculate each of the following areas and then calculate the number of tiles needed for that area.

EXAMPLE

A wall measures 3 m × 2.5 m.

This is 3 metres or 3000 millimetres high by 2.5 metres or 2500 millimetres wide. The tiles used are 150 mm × 150 mm.

STEP 1

Multiply the height of the wall by the length/width of the wall. This is the area of the wall.

Area of the wall = 3000 mm × 2500 mm = 7 500 000 mm².

STEP 2

Multiply the height of the tile by the width of the tile.

Area of the tile = 150 mm × 150 mm = 22 500 mm².

STEP 3

Divide the area of the wall by the area of the tiles.

Area of the wall divided by the area of the tile = 7 500 000 ÷ 22 500 = 334 tiles.

STEP 4

Add another 10% to allow for breakages/incorrect cuts. (10% rule is that the decimal is moved one place to the left.)

334 × 0.10 = 33.4 (33 tiles rounded down)

STEP 5

The final calculation for the number of tiles: 334 + 33 = 367 tiles.

STEP 6

Multiply the number of tiles by the cost of the tiles.

(The cost of the tiles could be per tile, per square metre or per carton or box of tiles. This will be specified in the question.)

QUESTION 1

A toilet floor is being re-tiled during a renovation. The floor measures 1.5 m × 1.0 m. The tiles being used are 300 mm × 300 mm quarry charcoal porcelain floor tiles and are on sale for $22.50 for a packet of eight tiles.

a Calculate the area of the floor.

Answer:

_____

b Calculate the area of the tiles.

Answer:

_____

c How many tiles are needed in total, including 10% for breakages?

Answer:

_____

_____

_____

d What is the cost of the tiles?

Answer:

_____

_____

QUESTION 2

A bathroom floor measures 2.5 m × 2.3 m. The tiles being used are 450 mm × 450 mm minima matt ceramic floor tiles and are priced at $37.50 for a packet of six tiles.

a Calculate the area of the floor.

Answer:

_____

b   Calculate the area of the tiles.

Answer:

_____

c   How many tiles are needed in total, including 10% for breakages?

Answer:

_____

_____

_____

d   What is the cost of the tiles?

Answer:

_____

_____

QUESTION 3

A laundry floor measures 3.15 m × 2.35 m. The tiles being used are 330 mm × 330 mm limestone ceramic matt floor tiles and are priced at $42.20 for a packet of 11 tiles.

a   Calculate the area of the floor.

Answer:

_____

b   Calculate the area of the tiles.

Answer:

_____

c   How many tiles are needed in total, including 10% for breakages?

Answer:

_____

_____

_____

d   What is the cost of the tiles?

Answer:

_____

_____

QUESTION 4

amanaimages/© Spaces Images/Blend Images

The floor of a bathroom measures 2.85 m × 2.75 m. The tiles being used are 200 mm × 200 mm white ceramic floor tiles and are priced at $1.12 each.

a   Calculate the area of the floor.

Answer:

_____

b   Calculate the area of the tiles.

Answer:

_____

c   How many tiles are needed in total, including 10% for breakages?

Answer:

_____

_____

_____

d   What is the cost of the tiles?

Answer:

_____

QUESTION 5

A bedroom floor measures 4.8 m × 4.6 m. The tiles being used are 300 mm × 600 mm wave-black floor tiles and are priced at $41.65 for a packet of six tiles.

a   Calculate the area of the floor.

Answer:

_____

b   Calculate the area of the tiles.

Answer:

_____

9780170474511

c How many tiles are needed in total, including 10% for breakages?

Answer:

d What is the cost of the tiles?

Answer:

QUESTION 6

The master bedroom floor (4.5 m × 4.4 m) and a smaller bedroom floor (2.9 m × 2.4 m) in a new house are being tiled. The tiles being used are 330 mm × 330 mm Thaicera terracotta ceramic floor tiles and are priced at $2.79 each.

a Calculate the area of both the bedroom floors.

Answer:

b Calculate the area of the tiles.

Answer:

c How many tiles are needed in total, including 10% for breakages?

Answer:

d What is the cost of the tiles?

Answer:

QUESTION 7

A dining room, kitchen, hallway and pantry floor are being tiled. The tiler estimates the total floor area is 15.5 m × 4.5 m. The tiles being used are 450 mm × 450 mm and are priced at $35.95 for a packet of six tiles.

a Calculate the area of the floor.

Answer:

b Calculate the area of the tiles.

Answer:

c How many tiles are needed in total, including 10% for breakages?

Answer:

d What is the cost of the tiles?

Answer:

QUESTION 8

A master bedroom, master bathroom, home office and living room need to be tiled. The total floor area is 18.75 m × 14.55 m. The tiles being used are 475 mm × 475 mm blue-grey slate self-stick vinyl tiles and are priced at $63.90 for a packet of 45 tiles.

a Calculate the area of the floor.

Answer:

b Calculate the area of the tiles.

Answer:

c How many tiles are needed in total, including 10% for breakages?

Answer:

d   What is the cost of the tiles?

Answer:

_____

_____

QUESTION 9

A tiler estimates the floor area of a two-storey, four bedroom house. She estimates the downstairs areas to be a total of 178.5 m². The upstairs areas are estimated to be a total of 155.8 m². The tiles being used are 475 mm × 475 mm travertine stone self-stick vinyl tiles and are priced at $71.20 for a packet of 16 tiles.

a   Add the downstairs and upstairs floor areas.

Answer:

_____

b   Calculate the area of the tiles.

Answer:

_____

c   How many tiles are needed in total, including 10% for breakages?

Answer:

_____

_____

_____

d   What is the cost of the tiles?

Answer:

_____

_____

QUESTION 10

A tiler estimates the floor area of a two-storey, two bedroom townhouse. He estimates the following measurements for the downstairs areas: living room is 4.25 m × 4.85 m, dining room is 3.35 m × 3.65 m, first bathroom is 3.15 m × 2.65 m and laundry is 2.55 m × 1.85 m. He estimates the following measurements for the upstairs areas: first bedroom is 3.4 m × 4.85 m, second bedroom is 3.55 m × 4.8 m and second bathroom is 3.65 m × 3.1 m. The tiles being used are 400 mm × 400 mm gloss Sorrento ceramic floor tiles and are priced at $40.37 for a packet of nine tiles.

a   Add the downstairs and upstairs floor areas.

Answer:

_____

_____

_____

_____

_____

_____

_____

_____

_____

b   Calculate the area of the tiles.

Answer:

_____

c   How many tiles are needed in total, including 10% for breakages?

Answer:

_____

_____

_____

d   What is the cost of the tiles?

Answer:

_____

_____

Unit 11: Earning Wages

Short-answer questions

Specific instructions to students

- This unit is designed to help you to calculate how much a job is worth and how long you need to complete the job.
- Read the questions below and answer all of them in the spaces provided.
- You may not use a calculator.
- You need to show all working.

QUESTION 1

A tiler works seven and a half hours per day. The pay rate is $39.31 per hour. How much is earned for the day, before tax?

Answer:

QUESTION 2

A labourer works seven and a half hours per day over five days. The pay rate is $22.50 per hour. How much is earned for the week, before tax?

Answer:

QUESTION 3

A tiler works a 36-hour week at an hourly rate of $39.31 and works for four hours on Saturday at double time. How much is earned for the week, before tax?

Answer:

QUESTION 4

A tiler charges an hourly rate of $45.50. She works for 36 hours over a week. How much does she earn each fortnight, before tax?

Answer:

QUESTION 5

A tiler gets paid monthly and works a total of 144 hours for the month. The hourly rate is $42.50. How much is earned for the month, before tax?

Answer:

QUESTION 6

A tiling contractor gets paid monthly and works a total of 144 hours every month at a rate of $44.50 per hour.

a   How much is the gross wage for the month?

Answer:

b   What is the gross yearly wage?

Answer:

QUESTION 7

Three casual tilers each work a total of 72 hours over a fortnight at a rate of $41.50 per hour. How much does their employer need to pay, in total, for the three wages, before tax?

Answer:

QUESTION 8

A tiler works 144 hours over a month, as per the normal hours required by the company employing him. The company pays an hourly rate of $39.50. Ten hours of overtime are also worked at double the hourly rate. How much is earned for the month, before tax?

Answer:

QUESTION 9

A tiler works 144 hours over a 20-day month. The company pays an hourly rate of $39.50. A rate of $39.30 per day is also paid for travel allowance for the 20 days. How much is earned for the month, before tax?

Answer:

QUESTION 10

iStockphoto/Larry Herfindal

A tiler works 72 hours over a 10-day fortnight. The company pays an hourly rate of $39.50. A rate of $39.30 per day is also paid for travel allowance for the 10 days. In addition, the tiler works two Saturdays for six hours each at double time. How much is earned for the month, before tax?

Answer:

9780170474511

Unit 12: Squaring Numbers

Section A: Introducing square numbers

Short-answer questions

Specific instructions to students

- This section is designed to help you to improve your skills and to increase your speed in squaring numbers.
- Read the questions below and answer all of them in the spaces provided.
- You may not use a calculator.
- You need to show all working.

Any number squared is multiplied by itself.

EXAMPLE

4 squared $= 4^2 = 4 \times 4 = 16$

QUESTION 1

$6^2 =$

Answer:

QUESTION 2

$8^2 =$

Answer:

QUESTION 3

$12^2 =$

Answer:

QUESTION 4

$3^2 =$

Answer:

QUESTION 5

$7^2 =$

Answer:

QUESTION 6

$11^2 =$

Answer:

QUESTION 7

$10^2 =$

Answer:

QUESTION 8

$9^2 =$

Answer:

QUESTION 9

$2^2 =$

Answer:

QUESTION 10

$14^2 =$

Answer:

Section B: Applying square numbers to the trade

Worded practical problems

Specific instructions to students

- This section is designed to help you to improve your skills and to increase your speed in calculating the volume of rectangular or square objects. The worded questions make the content relevant to everyday situations.
- Read the questions below and answer all of them in the spaces provided.
- You may not use a calculator.
- You need to show all working.

QUESTION 1

The floor of an ensuite measures 2.8 m × 2.8 m. What is the total area, in square metres?

Answer:

QUESTION 2

An outdoor area that will be tiled with polished porcelain tiles is 5.2 m × 5.2 m. What is the total area, in square metres?

Answer:

QUESTION 3

The dimensions of a bedroom floor being re-tiled are 3.6 m × 3.6 m. What is the total floor area to be tiled, in square metres?

Answer:

QUESTION 4

The backyard of a home is being transformed with a 'make over'. The yard's total area is 8 m × 8 m. The client wants an area left for lawn that measures 4.35 m × 4.35 m. The remaining area is being tiled. How much area is being tiled, in square metres?

Answer:

QUESTION 5

A house being built has a total floor area of 13.8 m × 13.8 m, which will be tiled. How much square area is the house?

Answer:

QUESTION 6

iStockphoto/Heidi van der Westhuizen

A shower recess measures 2.4 m × 2.4 m and is being jackhammered during a renovation to make way for a new concrete floor for tiling. The shower recess also joins onto a bedroom floor that measures 3.8 m × 3.8 m and is also being renovated and tiled. How many square metres in total are the two areas being tiled?

Answer:

9780170474511

QUESTION 7

During a renovation, a patio area and outdoor entertainment area are jackhammered and replaced with tiles. If the patio area is 3.8 m × 3.8 m and the outdoor entertainment area is 6.8 m × 6.8 m, how many square metres are being tiled?

Answer:

_____

QUESTION 8

A bathroom, dining room and kitchen are all being tiled. The bathroom area measures 2.5 m × 2.5 m. The total area of the dining room and the kitchen is 6.75 m × 6.75 m. The cost of the tiles that the client has chosen is $24.95 per m².

a   How many square metres are being tiled, in total?

Answer:

_____

b   What is the cost of the tiles?

Answer:

_____

QUESTION 9

Three areas are being renovated and re-tiled. Each area has different dimensions. The first area is a toilet that measures 1000 mm × 1800 mm. The second area is a laundry that measures 1000 mm × 2000 mm. The third area is a bathroom that measures 3000 mm × 2500 mm. The cost of the tiles is $34.95 per m².

a   How many square metres are being tiled, in total?

Answer:

_____

b   What is the total cost for the tiles?

Answer:

_____

QUESTION 10

A large two-storey, five bedroom house is being built and the client is keen to have polished porcelain tiles throughout all of the areas of the house. The total floor area to be tiled measures 59.5 m by 59.5 m. The cost of the tiles is $45.75 per m².

a   How many square metres are being tiled?

Answer:

_____

b   What is the total cost of the tiles?

Answer:

_____

Unit 13: Ratio Applications

EXAMPLE

The mixing ratio is 5 kg tile adhesive to 1.25 L of clean water.

QUESTION 1

Using the mixing ratio in the example box above, how much tile adhesive should be added to 1250 mL of clean water?

Answer:

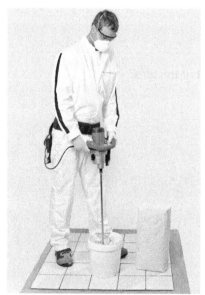

Shutterstock/CSImagemakers

QUESTION 2

Using the mixing ratio in the example box above, how much tile adhesive should be added to 630 mL of clean water?

Answer:

QUESTION 3

Using the mixing ratio in the example box on the left, how much tile adhesive should be added to 2.5 L of clean water?

Answer:

QUESTION 4

Using the mixing ratio in the example box on the left, how much tile adhesive should be added to 125 mL of clean water?

Answer:

QUESTION 5

Using the mixing ratio in the example box on the left, how much tile adhesive should be added to 300 mL of clean water?

Answer:

QUESTION 6

Using the mixing ratio in the example box on the left, how much tile adhesive should be added to 950 mL of clean water?

Answer:

QUESTION 7

Using the mixing ratio in the example box on the previous page, how much tile adhesive should be added to 3.75 L of clean water?

Answer:

_____

QUESTION 8

Using the mixing ratio in the example box on the previous page, how much tile adhesive should be added to 250 mL of clean water?

Answer:

_____

QUESTION 9

Using the mixing ratio in the example box on the previous page, how much tile adhesive should be added to 750 mL of clean water?

Answer:

_____

QUESTION 10

Using the mixing ratio in the example box on the previous page, how much tile adhesive should be added to 500 mL of clean water?

Answer:

_____

Section A: The apprentice years

Short-answer questions

Specific instructions to students

- This section is designed to help you to improve your Maths skills in the tiling trade.
- Read the questions below and answer all of them in the spaces provided.
- You may not use a calculator.
- You need to show all working.

QUESTION 1

A first-year apprentice tiler on a four-year apprenticeship gets paid $10.21 per hour. A travel allowance of $13.07 is also paid per day. If the apprentice works for 31 hours over four days, how much is earned for the working week, including allowances, before tax?

Answer:

_____

QUESTION 2

Shutterstock/Goodluz

A first-year apprentice tiler on a four-year apprenticeship gets paid $10.21 per hour. A travel allowance of $13.07 is also paid per day. If the apprentice works for 62 hours over an eight-day fortnight, how much is earned for the fortnight, including allowances, before tax?

Answer:

_____

QUESTION 3

A first-year apprentice tiler on a four-year apprenticeship gets paid $10.21 per hour. A travel allowance of $13.07 is also paid per day. If the apprentice works for 124 hours over a 16-day month, how much is earned for the month, including allowances, before tax?

Answer:

_____

QUESTION 4

A first-year apprentice tiler on a four-year apprenticeship gets paid $10.21 per hour. A travel allowance of $13.07 is also paid per day. The apprentice works for 31 hours over a four-day week. If $50 is spent on petrol, $38 on food and $57 on entertainment, how much money is left over?

Answer:

_____

QUESTION 5

A first-year apprentice tiler on a four-year apprenticeship gets paid $10.21 per hour, with an additional travel allowance of $13.01 per day. The apprentice works for 31 hours over a four-day week. If $35.50 is spent on petrol, $47.50 on food and $62.75 on entertainment, how much money is left over?

Answer:

_____

QUESTION 6

A second-year apprentice tiler on a four-year apprenticeship gets paid $12.19 per hour, plus $14.82 per day for a travel allowance. The apprentice works for 31 hours over a four-day week. How much is earned, including allowances, before tax?

Answer:

_____

QUESTION 7

A second-year apprentice tiler on a four-year apprenticeship gets paid $12.19 per hour, plus $14.82 per day for a travel allowance. The apprentice works for 62 hours over an eight-day fortnight. How much is earned, including allowances, before tax?

Answer:

_____

QUESTION 8

A second-year apprentice tiler on a four-year apprenticeship gets paid $12.19 per hour, plus $14.82 per day for a travel allowance. The apprentice works for 124 hours over a 16-day month. How much is earned, including allowances, before tax?

Answer:

QUESTION 9

A second-year apprentice tiler on a four-year apprenticeship gets paid $12.19 per hour, plus $14.82 per day for a travel allowance. The apprentice works for 31 hours over four days. If $86 is spent on tools, $49 on PPE gear and $18 on medical insurance, how much money is left?

Answer:

_____

QUESTION 10

A second-year apprentice tiler on a four-year apprenticeship gets paid $12.19 per hour, plus $14.82 per day for a travel allowance. The apprentice works for 62 hours over an eight-day fortnight. The apprentice's weekly expenses include: $45.50 for clothes, $42.90 for food and $180.50 for car registration. How much money is left after all the expenses?

Answer:

_____

Section B: Interpreting tables − Part I

Short-answer questions

Specific instructions to students

- This section is designed to help you to improve your Maths skills in the tiling trade.
- Read the questions below and answer all of them in the spaces provided.
- You may not use a calculator.
- You need to show all working.

The table below relates to the amount of grout required (kg/m²) for different tile sizes.

Tile size ($l \times w \times d$ mm)	Joint width (mm)		
	1.5	3.0	6.0
	Quantity of grout required (kg/m²)		
$50 \times 50 \times 6$	0.8	1.6	–
$100 \times 100 \times 6$	0.4	0.8	1.6
$150 \times 150 \times 6$	0.3	0.6	1.2
$200 \times 100 \times 10$	0.4	0.8	1.6
$300 \times 300 \times 6$	0.2	0.5	1.0

Use the information in the table on the previous page to answer the following questions.

QUESTION 1

If a tiler uses $150 \times 150 \times 6$ tiles with a joint width of 6 mm, how much grout is needed?

Answer:

_____

QUESTION 2

If a tiler uses $50 \times 50 \times 6$ tiles with a joint width of 3 mm, how much grout is needed?

Answer:

_____

QUESTION 3

If a tiler uses $300 \times 300 \times 6$ tiles with a joint width of 1.5 mm, how much grout is needed?

Answer:

_____

QUESTION 4

If a tiler uses $100 \times 100 \times 6$ tiles with a joint width of 3 mm, how much grout is needed?

Answer:

_____

QUESTION 5

If a tiler uses $200 \times 100 \times 10$ tiles with a joint width of 6 mm, how much grout is needed?

Answer:

_____

QUESTION 6

If a tiler uses $100 \times 100 \times 6$ tiles with a joint width of 1.5 mm, how much grout is needed?

Answer:

_____

QUESTION 7

If a tiler uses $300 \times 300 \times 6$ tiles with a joint width of 3 mm, how much grout is needed?

Answer:

_____

QUESTION 8

If a tiler uses $200 \times 100 \times 10$ tiles with a joint width of 1.5 mm, how much grout is needed?

Answer:

_____

QUESTION 9

If a tiler uses $300 \times 300 \times 6$ tiles with a joint width of 3 mm, how much grout is needed?

Answer:

_____

QUESTION 10

If a tiler uses $150 \times 150 \times 6$ tiles with a joint width of 6 mm, how much grout is needed?

Answer:

_____

9780170474511

Section C: Interpreting tables – Part II

Short-answer questions

Specific instructions to students

- This section is designed to help you to improve your Maths skills in the tiling trade.
- Read the questions below and answer all of them in the spaces provided.
- You may not use a calculator.
- You need to show all working.

The table below relates to the amount of grout required (kg/m^2) for different tile sizes.

Tile size ($l \times w \times d$ mm)	Joint width (mm)			
	1.5	3.0	5.0	8.0
	Quantity of grout required (kg/m^2)			
$25 \times 25 \times 4$	4.5	2.3	1.4	0.8
$100 \times 100 \times 8$	9.1	4.5	2.7	1.7
$200 \times 200 \times 8$	18.1	9.1	5.4	3.4
$330 \times 330 \times 9$	27.2	13.2	7.9	5.0

Use the above information to answer the following questions.

QUESTION 1

If a tiler uses $25 \times 25 \times 4$ tiles with a joint width of 5 mm, how much grout is needed?

Answer:

QUESTION 2

If a tiler uses $100 \times 100 \times 8$ tiles with a joint width of 3 mm, how much grout is needed?

Answer:

QUESTION 3

If a tiler uses $200 \times 200 \times 8$ tiles with a joint width of 1.5 mm, how much grout is needed?

Answer:

QUESTION 4

If a tiler uses $330 \times 330 \times 9$ tiles with a joint width of 3 mm, how much grout is needed?

Answer:

QUESTION 5

If a tiler uses $25 \times 25 \times 4$ tiles with a joint width of 1.5 mm, how much grout is needed?

Answer:

QUESTION 6

If a tiler uses $100 \times 100 \times 8$ tiles with a joint width of 8 mm, how much grout is needed?

Answer:

QUESTION 7

If a tiler uses $200 \times 200 \times 8$ tiles with a joint width of 3 mm, how much grout is needed?

Answer:

QUESTION 8

If a tiler uses $330 \times 330 \times 9$ tiles with a joint width of 8 mm, how much grout is needed?

Answer:

QUESTION 9

If a tiler uses 25 × 25 × 4 tiles with a joint width of 8 mm, how much grout is needed?

Answer:

QUESTION 10

If a tiler uses 200 × 200 × 8 tiles with a joint width of 8 mm, how much grout is needed?

Answer:

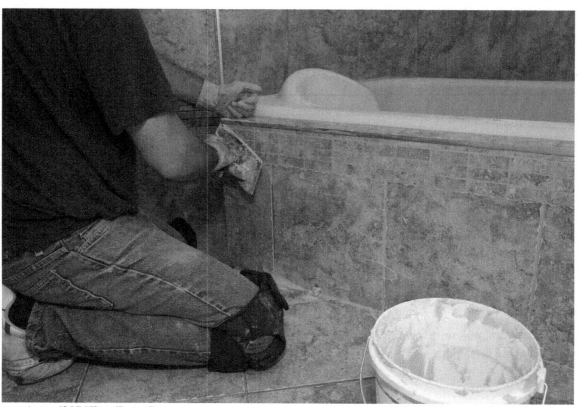

amanaimages/© LJM Photo/Design Pics

Tiling
Practice Written Exam for the Tiling Trade

Reading time: 10 minutes

Writing time: 1 hour 30 minutes

Section A: Literacy

Section B: General Mathematics

Section C: Trade Mathematics

QUESTION and ANSWER BOOK

Section	Topic	Number of questions	Marks
A	Literacy	7	22
B	General Mathematics	11	26
C	Trade Mathematics	44	52
		Total 62	**Total 100**

The sections may be completed in the order of your choice.

NO CALCULATORS are to be used during the exam.

Spelling

Read the passage below and then underline the 20 spelling errors.

10 marks

There are a few things to <u>remamber</u> when you are <u>geting</u> ready to lay tiles. The first step is to spread your <u>adhasive</u>. Make sure you don't spread the adhesive longer than a metre at any time because the adhesive may dry before you are ready to lay the tiles. The most common <u>aproach</u> is to set the <u>botom</u> two rows of tiles first. This provides a solid <u>foundasion</u> for the rest of the tiling. Once the first tile is <u>posisioned</u>, use a tile spacer to ensure enough room is left for grouting the side edge. The arm of the <u>spaser</u> should be positioned so that it leaves a gap between the tile you are laying and the tile that will go <u>diractly</u> above it. The tile should sit <u>aganst</u> the batten.

<u>Repeet</u> this process. Place the next tile and have your next spacer ready for <u>plasement</u>. When you begin a new row, ensure the tiles are sitting against the <u>baten</u> and the tiles are <u>seperated</u> with a spacer at the top of each corner. Continue laying the tiles along the batten until the row is <u>complate</u>. The next row can then be started. From the first tile, the second row can be started; <u>howevar</u>, remember to use spacers at the top of each tile.

It is important to keep checking the tiling as it <u>progreses</u>. Check the levels on <u>evary</u> row by using a spirit level or a straight edge. <u>Occasionaly</u>, a tile may need to be removed and flattened before continuing.

Tiles can be arranged horizontally or <u>verticaly</u>.

Correct the spelling errors by writing them out with the correct spelling below.

remember, getting, adhesive, approach, bottom, foundation, positioned, spacer, directly, against, repeat, placement,

batten, separated, complete, however, progresses, every, occasionally, vertically

Alphabetising

Put the following words into alphabetical order.

Terracotta	Timber batten
Straight edge	Sealant
Floor leveller	Masking tape
Tile spacers	Mosaic tiles
Ceramic	Shower hob
Grout	Bucket
Tile adhesive	Spatula

Bucket

Ceramic

Floor leveller

Grout

Masking tape

Mosaic tiles

Sealant

Shower hob

Spatula

Straight edge

Terracotta

Tile adhesive

Tile spacers

Timber batten

Comprehension

Short-answer questions

Specific instructions to students

- Read the following passage and answer the questions using full sentences.

Bill and Jen are considering tiles for their bathroom, so they decide to ask for some advice. They visit a tiling store and ask one of the consultants, Fiona, about any tips, hints or things to keep in mind when selecting tiles and laying the tiles. Fiona tells them 'When you choose your tiles, it is important to calculate a $2-3$ mm allowance for grout gaps between the tiles. The tiling process is always the same, no matter what pattern you decide to lay your tiles in.'

Fiona also suggests 'Before you start tiling, ensure that the surface is clean. If the surface is particularly dusty, you might like to seal it with a coat of PVA glue before.'

Jen asks 'If we have finished laying our tiles, will we need to trim the tiles at both ends of the wall? I know that it's a little bit of extra work but will it make the tiling look neater, once we've finished the job?' 'It sure will!' answers Fiona.

Jen also asks 'If we tile a ledge or above a basin, should we start tiling in the middle?' Fiona responds 'Yes, I think this would probably give you a more balanced end result.'

'Is there any other advice you could possibly offer us?' asks Jen. 'Make sure that you use a notched spreader because that will help to get a consistent depth of adhesive overall. If you decide to tile the underside of a ledge and you have finished sticking down the lines, it would be a good idea to prop up a flat board under them just to keep them in place', offers Fiona.

'Do you have any advice about grouting?' Bill enquires.

'Well, if you're thinking about grouting a large area, make sure that you use a rubber float and start in the bottom corner, then push the grout upwards and then across. It's also a good idea to sweep down diagonally just to remove any excess. You can then work upwards again and start going across. Just keep going until you reach the corner that is the furthest away' Fiona says.

QUESTION 1 — 1 mark

According to Fiona, what is important for Bill and Jen to remember when they are choosing their tiles?

Answer:

Remember to allow approximately 2−3 mm for the gaps for grout.

QUESTION 2 — 1 mark

What does Fiona suggest as a solution to sealing dusty surfaces?

Answer:

Seal with a coat of PVA glue before tiling.

QUESTION 3 — 1 mark

What is the purpose of trimming the tiles at both ends of the wall once they are laid?

Answer:

It makes the final finish look neater.

QUESTION 4 — 1 mark

Why does using a notched spreader assist the process of laying tiles?

Answer:

It gives an even spread of the tile adhesive.

QUESTION 5 — 1 mark

What process does Fiona suggest for completing grouting?

Answer:

Use a rubber float and start in the bottom corner, then push the grout upwards and across. Sweep down diagonally to remove any excess and then work upwards again and across. Continue this process until you reach the corner that is the furthest away.

Section B: General Mathematics

QUESTION 1 — 1 + 1 + 1 = 3 marks

What unit of measurement is used to measure:

a the perimeter of an area for tiling?

Answer:

Millimetres, metres or centimetres

b the amount of grout required?

Answer:

Grams or kilograms

c an area of a wall for tiling?

Answer:

Square metres (m²)

QUESTION 2 — 1 + 1 + 1 = 3 marks

Give examples of how the following might be used in the tiling trade.

a Percentage

Answer:

Allowance for extra tiles/breakages

b Decimals

Answer:

Measurement of width of a wall or floor

c Fraction

Answer:

Grout mix

QUESTION 3   1 + 1 = 2 marks

Convert the following units.

a   1 kg to grams

Answer:

1000 g

b   1500 g to kilograms

Answer:

1.5 kg

QUESTION 4   2 marks

Write the following in descending order.

0.7   0.71   7.1   70.1   701.00   7.0

Answer:

701.00, 70.1, 7.1, 7.0, 0.71, 0.7

QUESTION 5   1 + 1 = 2 marks

Write the decimal number that is between:

a   0.1 and 0.2

Answer:

0.15

b   1.3 and 1.4

Answer:

1.35

QUESTION 6   1 + 1 = 2 marks

Round off the following numbers to two (2) decimal places.

a   5.177

Answer:

5.18

b   12.655

Answer:

12.66

QUESTION 7   1 + 1 = 2 marks

Estimate the following by approximation.

a 101×81

Answer:

8000

b 399×21

Answer:

8000

QUESTION 8   1 + 1 = 2 marks

What do the following add up to?

a $25, $13.50 and $165.50

Answer:

$204

b $4, $5.99 and $229.50

Answer:

$239.49

QUESTION 9   1 + 1 = 2 marks

Subtract the following.

a   196 from 813

Answer:

617

b   5556 from 9223

Answer:

3667

QUESTION 10   1 + 1 = 2 marks

Use division to solve the following.

a $4824 \div 3 =$

Answer:

1608

b $84.2 \div 0.4 =$

Answer:

210.5

QUESTION 11   2 + 2 = 4 marks

Using BODMAS, solve the following.

a $(3 \times 7) \times 4 + 9 - 5 =$

Answer:

88

b $(8 \times 12) \times 2 + 8 - 4 =$

Answer:

196

Section C: Trade Mathematics

Basic Operations

Addition

QUESTION 1   1 mark

A tiler purchases 36 20-kg containers of tile adhesive, 144 450 mm × 450 mm ceramic floor tiles and 15 4-L containers of floor leveller. How many items have been purchased in total?

Answer:

195 items

QUESTION 2   1 mark

A tiler purchases two floats for $25, PPE gear for $45 and a spirit level for $17. What is the total cost?

Answer:

$87

Subtraction

QUESTION 1   1 mark

A tiler cuts off 90 mm from a ceramic floor tile that measures 450 mm. How many millimetres remain of the tile?

Answer:

360 mm

QUESTION 2   1 mark

An apprentice purchases PPE gear and the total comes to $124. The manager of the shop takes off a discount of $35 during a sale. How much does the apprentice pay?

Answer:

$89

Multiplication

QUESTION 1   1 mark

An apprentice shifts five pallets of 15-kg multi-purpose floor leveller. Each pallet has 36 bags on it. How many bags are on the five pallets, in total?

Answer:

180 bags

QUESTION 2   1 mark

A tiling contractor uses 250 10-L containers of tile adhesive in the first month, 200 10-L containers in the second month and 160 10-L containers in the third month. How many 10-L containers have been used, in total?

Answer:

610

Division

QUESTION 1   1 mark

An invoice for a completed tiling job comes to $5578, which is the cost of labour and materials. If the work took six days to complete, what is the average cost per day for labour and materials?

Answer:

$929.67

QUESTION 2   1 mark

At a yearly stocktake at a tile store, a store person counts 72 containers of 4-L floor leveller. If 12 containers are packed onto each pallet, how many pallets are there?

Answer:

6

Decimals

Addition

QUESTION 1   1 mark

An apprentice purchases a grout tool for $39.95, three 63-mm diamond blades for $62.50 and a tile cutter for $154.50. How much is charged for the purchase?

Answer:

$256.95

QUESTION 2   1 mark

An online store sells two packets of 11 ceramic floor tiles for $79.95, a tile laser for $111.50 and five bags of 5-kg coloured grout for $112.85. What is the total cost for the items?

Answer:

$304.30

Subtraction

QUESTION 1   1 mark

A casual labourer working with a tiler earns $418.50 for two days of work. He spends $35.95 on clothes and $25.50 on food. How much money is left?

Answer:

$357.05

QUESTION 2   1 mark

A supervisor of a tiling company purchases a blue steel wheelbarrow for $124.50. If it is paid for with three $50 notes, how much change is given?

Answer:

$25.50

Multiplication

QUESTION 1   2 marks

A tiling contractor buys three spinner floats for $37.95 each at a sale.

a   How much does it cost for the three floats?

Answer:

$113.85

b   How much change is given from $150.00?

Answer:

$36.15

QUESTION 2   2 marks

Four packets of seven 300 mm × 300 mm ceramic floor tiles are purchased at a cost of $28.50 each.

a   How much does it cost for the tiles?

Answer:

$114

b   How much change is given from $120.00?

Answer:

$6 change

Division

QUESTION 1   1 mark

A tiler earns $987.00 for five days of work. How much is earned per day?

Answer:

$197.40 per day

QUESTION 2   1 mark

Four 355 mm × 100 mm pointed floor trowels cost $88.80. What is the cost of each?

Answer:

$22.20 each

Fractions

QUESTION 1   1 mark

$\frac{1}{4} + \frac{1}{2} =$

Answer:

$\frac{3}{4}$

QUESTION 2   1 mark

$\frac{4}{5} - \frac{1}{3} =$

Answer:

$\frac{7}{15}$

QUESTION 3   1 mark

$\frac{2}{3} \times \frac{1}{4} =$

Answer:

$\frac{2}{12}$ or $\frac{1}{6}$

QUESTION 4   1 mark

$\frac{3}{4} \div \frac{1}{2} =$

Answer:

$1\frac{2}{4}$ or $1\frac{1}{2}$

Percentages

Calculating extra tiles for breakages/cutting/possible wastage

QUESTION 1   1 mark

A tiler adds 10% to the amount of tiles required, to allow for breakages. If 249 tiles are required, how many should be added for breakages? (Round up)

Answer:

25 tiles

QUESTION 2   1 mark

A tiler adds 10% to the amount of tiles required, to allow for breakages. If 187 tiles are required, how many should be added for breakages? (Round up)

Answer:

19 tiles

Percentages and purchasing

QUESTION 1   1 mark

A hardware store has a '10% off' sale on all tiling tools. If a customer's purchase totals $149.00, what is the final price once 10% has been taken off?

Answer:

$134.10

QUESTION 2   1 mark

Tiling products are discounted by 20% in a specialist tiling store. If the regular retail price is $120.00, how much does the customer pay after the discount?

Answer:

$96.00

Measurement Conversions

QUESTION 1   1 mark

How many grams are in a 5-kg bag of coloured grout?

Answer:

5000 g

QUESTION 2   1 mark

How many centimetres are in 35 mm?

Answer:

3.5 cm

Measurement

Area

QUESTION 1   1 mark

Calculate the perimeter of a patio being tiled that measures 13 m × 3 m.

Answer:

32 m

QUESTION 2   1 mark

Determine the perimeter of an outdoor area that measures 5.4 m × 5.7 m.

Answer:

22.2 m

Costings

QUESTION 1   1 mark

The outdoor entertainment area being tiled at the back of a house measures 5 m × 6 m. What is the total outdoor area?

Answer:

30 m²

QUESTION 2   1 mark

Calculate the total wall area of a shower that measures 12 m × 11 m.

Answer:

132 m²

Advanced costings

QUESTION 1   1 mark

A lounge room measures 5 m × 6 m. The client wants to use 200 mm × 200 mm white ceramic floor tiles, which cost $30.00 per square metre. What is the total cost of the tiles?

Answer:

$900.00

QUESTION 2   1 mark

A living room measures 5.5 m × 5.5 m. The client wants to use 450 mm × 450 mm stone pattern floor tiles, which cost $14.50 per square metre. What is the total cost for the tiles?

Answer:

$438.63

Earning Wages

QUESTION 1   1 mark

A tiler works a 36-hour week at an hourly rate of $39.31. How much is earned for the week, before tax?

Answer:

$1415.16

QUESTION 2   1 mark

A tiler works 144 hours over a month. The hourly rate is $39.31. How much is earned for the month, before tax?

Answer:

$5660.64

9780170474511

Squaring numbers

Introducing square numbers

QUESTION 1   1 mark

What is 7^2?

Answer:

49

QUESTION 2   1 mark

A dining room floor area measures 13 m × 13 m and is being tiled with 450 mm × 450 mm ceramic floor tiles. What is the total floor area?

Answer:

169 m²

Applying square numbers to the trade

QUESTION 1   2 marks

A patio area measures 6.4 m × 6.4 m. What is the total area, in square metres?

Answer:

40.96 m²

QUESTION 2   2 marks

An outdoor entertainment area measures 5.3 m × 5.3 m and is being tiled with 600 mm × 600 mm white ceramic tiles. What is the total outdoor area?

Answer:

28.09 m²

Ratio Applications

QUESTION 1   2 marks

Using the mixing ratio of 5 kg of tile adhesive to 1.25 L of water, how much tile adhesive should be added to 1250 mL of clean water?

Answer:

5 kg

QUESTION 2   2 marks

Using the mixing ratio of 5 kg of tile adhesive to 1.25 L of water, how much tile adhesive should be added to approximately 612 mL of clean water?

Answer:

2.5 kg

Applying Maths to the Tiling Trade

The apprentice years

QUESTION 1   1 mark

A first-year apprentice tiler gets paid $10.21 per hour. If the apprentice works for 31 hours over four days, what is the gross pay?

Answer:

$316.51

QUESTION 2   1 mark

A first-year apprentice tiler gets paid $10.21 per hour. If the apprentice works for 62 hours over a fortnight, what is the gross pay?

Answer:

$633.02

Interpreting tables

Tile size ($l \times w \times d$ mm)	Joint width (mm)		
	1.5	3.0	6.0
	Quantity of grout required (kg/m²)		
$50 \times 50 \times 6$	0.8	1.6	–
$100 \times 100 \times 6$	0.4	0.8	1.6
$150 \times 150 \times 6$	0.3	0.6	1.2
$200 \times 100 \times 10$	0.4	0.8	1.6
$300 \times 300 \times 6$	0.2	0.5	1.0

Use the above information to answer the following questions.

QUESTION 1   2 marks

If a tiler uses $150 \times 150 \times 6$ tiles with a joint width of 3 mm, how much grout is needed?

Answer:

0.6 kg/m²

QUESTION 2   2 marks

If a tiler uses $300 \times 300 \times 6$ tiles with a joint width of 1.5 mm, how much grout is needed?

Answer:

0.2 kg/m²

9780170474511

Glossary

Adhesive   Used to stick tiles to a surface.

Bed   The layer of adhesive or mortar that the tiles are laid onto.

Body   The material that the tile is made up of, not taking the glaze into account.

Buttering   The spreading of a bond coat to the back of a tile. This process is undertaken directly before the tile is set or placed.

Ceramic tile   These are generally known as glazed tiles and they can be used for either or both wall and floor applications.

Diagonal set   Tile set at a 45° angle to the wall.

Efflorescence   A crystal-like crust that forms on the surface of grout or unglazed tiles when moisture reacts with impurities within the mortar.

Finishes   The textural or visual characteristics of a tile's surface.

Fluted tiles   These tiles have a ridged surface, making them slip-resistant.

Format   This term refers to the size of any tile. Tiles sizes vary greatly, ranging from small mosaic tiles to large tiles.

Glaze   A type of clear coating that is fired or fused onto the ceramic tile body. Once a tile is glazed, the surface is smooth and waterproof.

Glazed porcelain   This type of tile is considered to be the most commonly used indoor floor tile. Glazed porcelain tiles are characterised by their density and strength.

Grout joint   The space left between tiles, which is filled with grout. Normal joint widths are 3 mm; however, this may vary depending on the client's choice of finish.

Mosaic tiles   Because of their small size, mosaic tiles are usually attached to a mesh backing, for easy installation. Mosaic tiles are commonly made of glass, stone or pebbles.

Porosity   The likelihood of a tile absorbing moisture.

Quarry tiles   Tiles made from naturally occurring clay. They can be glazed or unglazed.

Screed   A sand or cement mixture used to level out uneven concrete flooring prior to tiling.

Sealers/Sealants   Unglazed floor tiles need a clear coat so as to protect the surface from any range of grease spills or staining.

Slip-resistant tiles   This term refers to tiles that have been treated so as to prevent slipping.

Terracotta   Tiles made from traditional clay. Usually cream or red in colour, terracotta tiles can have a smooth, polished or rustic finish.

Wastage   When calculating the amount of tiles required for a job, 10% is usually added to allow for wastage due to cutting and/or breakages.

Water absorption   Tiles are porous by nature and naturally absorb moisture. Water absorption is measured as a percentage of the dry tile weight.

Formulae and Data

Area

Area = length × breadth and is given in square units
$Area = l \times b$

Perimeter

Perimeter is the length of all sides added together.
Perimeter = length + breadth + length + breadth
$Perimeter = l + b + l + b$

9780170474511

Times Tables

1

1 × 1	=	1
2 × 1	=	2
3 × 1	=	3
4 × 1	=	4
5 × 1	=	5
6 × 1	=	6
7 × 1	=	7
8 × 1	=	8
9 × 1	=	9
10 × 1	=	10
11 × 1	=	11
12 × 1	=	12

2

1 × 2	=	2
2 × 2	=	4
3 × 2	=	6
4 × 2	=	8
5 × 2	=	10
6 × 2	=	12
7 × 2	=	14
8 × 2	=	16
9 × 2	=	18
10 × 2	=	20
11 × 2	=	22
12 × 2	=	24

3

1 × 3	=	3
2 × 3	=	6
3 × 3	=	9
4 × 3	=	12
5 × 3	=	15
6 × 3	=	18
7 × 3	=	21
8 × 3	=	24
9 × 3	=	27
10 × 3	=	30
11 × 3	=	33
12 × 3	=	36

4

1 × 4	=	4
2 × 4	=	8
3 × 4	=	12
4 × 4	=	16
5 × 4	=	20
6 × 4	=	24
7 × 4	=	28
8 × 4	=	32
9 × 4	=	36
10 × 4	=	40
11 × 4	=	44
12 × 4	=	48

5

1 × 5	=	5
2 × 5	=	10
3 × 5	=	15
4 × 5	=	20
5 × 5	=	25
6 × 5	=	30
7 × 5	=	35
8 × 5	=	40
9 × 5	=	45
10 × 5	=	50
11 × 5	=	55
12 × 5	=	60

6

1 × 6	=	6
2 × 6	=	12
3 × 6	=	18
4 × 6	=	24
5 × 6	=	30
6 × 6	=	36
7 × 6	=	42
8 × 6	=	48
9 × 6	=	54
10 × 6	=	60
11 × 6	=	66
12 × 6	=	72

7

1 × 7	=	7
2 × 7	=	14
3 × 7	=	21
4 × 7	=	28
5 × 7	=	35
6 × 7	=	42
7 × 7	=	49
8 × 7	=	56
9 × 7	=	63
10 × 7	=	70
11 × 7	=	77
12 × 7	=	84

8

1 × 8	=	8
2 × 8	=	16
3 × 8	=	24
4 × 8	=	32
5 × 8	=	40
6 × 8	=	48
7 × 8	=	56
8 × 8	=	64
9 × 8	=	72
10 × 8	=	80
11 × 8	=	88
12 × 8	=	96

9

1 × 9	=	9
2 × 9	=	18
3 × 9	=	27
4 × 9	=	36
5 × 9	=	45
6 × 9	=	54
7 × 9	=	63
8 × 9	=	72
9 × 9	=	81
10 × 9	=	90
11 × 9	=	99
12 × 9	=	108

10

1 × 10	=	10
2 × 10	=	20
3 × 10	=	30
4 × 10	=	40
5 × 10	=	50
6 × 10	=	60
7 × 10	=	70
8 × 10	=	80
9 × 10	=	90
10 × 10	=	100
11 × 10	=	110
12 × 10	=	120

11

1 × 11	=	11
2 × 11	=	22
3 × 11	=	33
4 × 11	=	44
5 × 11	=	55
6 × 11	=	66
7 × 11	=	77
8 × 11	=	88
9 × 11	=	99
10 × 11	=	110
11 × 11	=	121
12 × 11	=	132

12

1 × 12	=	12
2 × 12	=	24
3 × 12	=	36
4 × 12	=	48
5 × 12	=	60
6 × 12	=	72
7 × 12	=	84
8 × 12	=	96
9 × 12	=	108
10 × 12	=	120
11 × 12	=	132
12 × 12	=	144

Multiplication Grid

	1	2	3	4	5	6	7	8	9	10	11	12
1	1	2	3	4	5	6	7	8	9	10	11	12
2	2	4	6	8	10	12	14	16	18	20	22	24
3	3	6	9	12	15	18	21	24	27	30	33	36
4	4	8	12	16	20	24	28	32	36	40	44	48
5	5	10	15	20	25	30	35	40	45	50	55	60
6	6	12	18	24	30	36	42	48	54	60	66	72
7	7	14	21	28	35	42	49	56	63	70	77	84
8	8	16	24	32	40	48	56	64	72	80	88	96
9	9	18	27	36	45	54	63	72	81	90	99	108
10	10	20	30	40	50	60	70	80	90	100	110	120
11	11	22	33	44	55	66	77	88	99	110	121	132
12	12	24	36	48	60	72	84	96	108	120	132	144

9780170474511

Notes

Notes

Notes

Notes

9780170474511